Lyman C. Smith

Mabel Gray And Other Poems

Lyman C. Smith

Mabel Gray And Other Poems

ISBN/EAN: 9783744714310

Printed in Europe, USA, Canada, Australia, Japan

Cover: Foto ©Thomas Meinert / pixelio.de

More available books at **www.hansebooks.com**

MABEL GRAY

And Other Poems

BY

LYMAN C. SMITH

❋

TORONTO

WILLIAM BRIGGS

WESLEY BUILDINGS

Montreal: C. W. COATES | Halifax: S. F. HUESTIS

1896

THE soaring lark from swelling breast may sound

   Exultant strains that thrill the world below ;

   The thrush on flute melodious may blow

The sweet sad tones that stir the soul profound ;

But haply, too, on lonely shady mound

   The wood-bird pipes a heart-song soft and low,

   That through her own breast sends a cheery glow,

Yet brightens, too, the little world around :

And may not one who feels his bosom swell

   And thrill at every note sublime and strong,

Who loves the sweet sad melodies that dwell

   And linger in the heart's recesses long,

The while himself he cheers, attempt as well

   To lighten others with his artless song ?

Contents.

MABEL GRAY,

AND OTHER POEMS.

———

Mabel Gray.

WHERE on one of England's manors
Last at even fell the sunbeams,
  Ashley Lodge in silence lay ;
At the vale and hillside's meeting,
Where first crept the stealthy shadows
From their noontide hiding-places,
  Was the home of Mabel Gray.

Ashley Lodge lay wrapped in silence,
For the master from its portals
  Death had beckoned years before :
Lady Ashley with her children
Left the home where every turning
Brought remembrance of the loved one
  Who should tread its walks no more.

MABEL GRAY.

Tenant farmers tilled the manor;
One of these was Mabel's father.
  There was not a sloping green,
Not a grove with beck'ning branches,
Not a dell with happy flowers
Met to slumber, that in childhood
  Mabel's footprints had not seen.

There was not a tripping brooklet ,
By whose side she had not rambled,
  Prattling to its prattling tide ;
By it stood no timid lily
Bowing, gazing at its image
Mirrored in the crystal water,
  That from Mabel's glance could hide.

Known in every tenant's cottage,
They had called her " Happy Mabel,"
  For her heart seemed ever gay ;
At her coming came a brightness
Such as when a troop of sunbeams
Sudden peep in at the window
  On a clouded autumn day.

As she rambled gathering flowers
By life's wayside, more a woman's,
  Less a child's, her bearing grew.
On she followed in the pathway
Till the sunny land of childhood
Lay behind her, and before her
  That of womanhood in view.

Was this " Happy Mabel " pretty?
If a brow of new-born snowflakes,
  Lustrous eyes of liquid brown,
Tresses such as ever England
Gives to all her fairest maidens,
Tresses lit with lurking sunbeams,
  Ample tresses, flowing down;

Lips whose tintings filled with envy
Even England's bright-lipped roses;
  Cheeks of lustre rich and rare;
If these, with the grace of flowers
Waltzing with the playful zephyrs,—
If these make a maiden pretty,
  Then was " Happy Mabel " fair.

Near her home a tree stood, shading
With its boughs a bank of mosses,
   At whose foot a streamlet crept.
Often here the voice of Mabel
Softly on the air of ev'ning
Poured its richness, while her fingers
   Swiftly o'er the lutestring swept.

Here one summer ev'ning seated
Singing to her lute, a footstep
   Heard she coming on the way.
Looking up she saw approaching,
Wearied, stained with dust, a stripling.
Near he came, and, pausing by her,
   Bowed and asked for Farmer Gray.

Soon he found the rugged farmer,
Stated that he wished employment,
   That he had the country sought,
For he wearied of the clamor
Of his home, the busy city ;
Willing were his hands to labor,
   Though of farm work knew he naught.

MABEL GRAY.

By his frankness pleased, the farmer
Gave the city youth employment
　　With his workmen, day by day.
At the failures and the blunders
Of the struggling town-bred stripling,
At the jests they played upon him,
　　Many a hearty laugh had they.

But he struggled on in patience,
Laughed with others at his blunders,
　　Till, when two years' time was o'er,
"There is not," the farmer boasted,
"There is not on all the manor
One so trusty, one so skilful,
　　One to equal Evan Moore."

Mild blue eyes, that fell if noticed,
Mabel oft saw bent upon her
　　Whene'er Evan Moore was nigh.
Once, while both alone, she sudden
Grew indignant and demanded
Why her every step and motion
　　Must be followed by his eye.

" 'Tis because it tells," he answered,
" Where my feet would gladly follow ;
   Fault of mine you had not known,
If your own had not been guilty."
Mabel lost her indignation,
And confessed, though not in language,
   Hers were guilty as his own.

Near her home that tree stood, shading
With its boughs a bank of mosses,
   Near whose foot a streamlet crept.
Often here the voice of Mabel
Softly on the air of ev'ning
Blent with Evan's, while her fingers
   Swiftly o'er the lutestring swept.

Time went dancing by on tiptoe,
Pointing to a happy future
   Strewn with blossoms all the way ;
But at last one summer morning
Suddenly there came a parting ;
Evan had a note demanding
   His return without delay.

So they parted; but he promised
At the autumn's second coming
  To return his bride to claim.
Thus in hope but yet in sadness
Parted they, and much he warned her
Lest another might deprive him
  Of his treasure ere he came.

Summer passed and golden autumn;
Spring now over hill and meadow
  Had her vernal mantle flung.
Often to that bed of mosses
Mabel, at the hour of ev'ning,
Stole and to her lute repeated
  Songs she had with Evan sung.

Thus one ev'ning seated singing,
Looking up she saw a horseman
  Near her, list'ning to her lay.
Mabel, startled at his presence,
Sudden ceased; and then the horseman
Seeing that he had been noticed,
  Bowed his thanks and rode away.

Soon there came a message saying
Ashley Lodge was now refitted,
  And the former master's son
Had returned from home ancestral ;
That the tenants of the manor
Were to Ashley Lodge invited
  On the morrow, every one.

Happy was the tenants' meeting
With the son of former master
  Cherished still in many a heart.
Song of youth and laugh of children
Echoed through the shaded pathways,
And Night's ebon pinions only
  Forced the joyous ones to part.

Mabel, in the youthful Ashley
Recognized the list'ning horseman ;
  Ashley, too, the singer knew,
And to hear that song repeated
Oft he found his feet were straying
When a dusky veil of silence
  Night upon the valley threw.

Near her home that tree stood, shading
With its boughs a bank of mosses,
    Near whose foot a streamlet crept.
Often there the voice of Mabel
Softly on the air of ev'ning
Blent with Ashley's, while her fingers
    Swiftly o'er the lutestring swept.

Summer was about departing;
Glimpses of the robes of autumn
    Were upon the hilltop seen.
Ashley took the hand of Mabel,
Said that one thing yet was lacking
In his home, and then he asked her
    If she there would reign as queen.

Mabel, startled at his question,
Said she was not bred a lady;
    It would wound the Ashley pride
If the daughter of a tenant,
Bred to labor from her cradle,
Ignorant of courtly manners,
    Should presume to be his bride.

Ashley to her would not listen,
But asserted that her presence
   Would the proudest home adorn.
So at last the maiden yielded ;
Seemingly she had forgotten
All the vows she made to Evan
   On that parting summer morn.

Autumn came with rustling garments,
And with ev'ning's dusky shadows,
   Came at last her Evan Moore.
Weary though he seemed with walking,
Covered with the dust of travel,
Mabel scarcely rose to greet him
   As he reached the cottage door.

Evan straightway told his errand—
This was autumn's second coming :
   He was here to claim his bride.
Mabel told him all the story
Of her plighted word to Ashley,
How she pleaded her unfitness,
   How he every word denied.

Evan bitterly reproached her.
" Dazzled by his courtly manners,
    Then you have forsaken me.
You have every promise broken
Made to me that summer morning ;
You have all your vows forgotten.
    Is *this* woman's constancy ?"

Mabel at his words reproachful
Only smiled, and then asserted
    She was constant as before.
Then she, laughing, told him plainly
His deception was a failure—
She had in the courtly Ashley
    Recognized her Evan Moore.

" By your eyes of blue I knew you
When that ev'ning here to listen
    You with horseman's trappings came.
Were I wrapt in death's deep slumber,
And those eyes should bend upon me,
Mine would waken from their slumber,
    And my lips should breathe your name."

2

Now in Ashley Lodge walks Mabel ;
England boasts no form more queenly
   'Mong her noble dames of yore ;
Not a happier home than Mabel's,
Not a prouder man than Ashley.
Mabel yet in playful humor
   Often calls him Evan Moore.

Known in every tenant's cottage,
Still they call her " Happy Mabel,"
   For her heart seems ever gay ;
At her coming comes a brightness
Such as when a troop of sunbeams
Sudden peep in at the window
   On a clouded autumn day.

Constancy.

I DREAMED a friend and I together strayed
   In gardens wide, where grove and gay parterre
Lay side by side, and fountains idly tossed
   Their jewelled droplets in the morning air.

To me, the form of this friend worthy seemed
   Of all the praise that beauty e'er should win.
Perchance I thought it such because I knew
   The beauty of the soul that dwelt within.

We paused to rest within a latticed bower.
   Though leafy vines had thick o'erspread the whole,
Eaves-dropping roses panting bosoms pressed
   Against the bars and hurried glances stole.

The gate was near.   I asked if she would tread
   With me the path that wound o'er plain and hill.
She raised her trusting eyes and grasped my hand
   So warmly that I feel it clasping still.

I plucked a list'ning rose and gave it her;
   Then, passing out, an altar we espied
Beside the gate. We knelt and vowed that naught
   Should ever lead one from the other's side.

Our way seemed clothed in nature's loveliness.
   Green groves and sunny valleys smiled to greet
Our coming; gaily brooklets leaped and danced,
   And flowers cast their garments at our feet.

But soon the path grew steep and rough; the hills
   And dales no more in sunny robes were dressed.
The weary foot by jagged cliff was bruised,
   And blasts with wintry arrows pierced the breast.

Then I reproached myself that I had led
   Her with me o'er this pathway rough and cold;
But, turning, met the same calm, trusting eyes,
   And found her hand had not relaxed its hold.

We passed the mount and found a desert plain
   Where reveled sultry winds. We long had strayed
Its trackless wastes, when suddenly we saw
   A river far ahead and palm-tree shade.

Our hearts took courage at the welcome sight.
　We hastened to the river, but I sank
Oppressed with heat and faint from weariness,
　Just as we reached the palm-trees on its bank.

Then while my wearied frame and throbbing brain
　Foretold the near approach of death's dark hour,
Again I bitterly reproached myself
　That I had led her from her garden bower.

I felt her cooling hand upon my brow ;
　My flitting spirit, turning, saw her press
My parted lips, then close my eyes and sit,
　Still clinging to my hand, in silentness.

Years passed.　My soul came back and saw
　Her by a mound whose marble bore my name,
Her eyes bent on a faded garden rose,
　Their pure and trusting love light still the same.

Aner and Gyne.

UPON the earth the gods yet walked, and flung
  With lavish hands their gifts on every side ;
The bending bough with luscious fruitage hung,
  And flowers marked their footprints far and wide.
Primeval man they formed ; in him combined
  Both shape and radiant beauty like their own,
And each bestowed some treasure of the mind,
  Till all their graces dwelt in him alone.
They loved the creature they had formed, and sought
  To make an earthly heaven of his home,
Where from their mansions, bright with gold in-
      wrought,
  They might descend and daily with him roam,
To show him all the riches of the earth,
  The varied wealth of beauty it possessed,
Unfold his godlike mind, and wake to birth
  The slumbering emotions of his breast.

In Greece they chose his home, and hand in hand
  Would wander at his side, as friend with friend,

'Mid all the new-born glories of that land
    Whose charms for mortal eye shall never end.
They strayed by streams where mossy bank beguiles
    To cooling rest 'neath overarching tree ;
Together climbed her cliffs, and saw the isles
    Of marble breast that dot her silver sea.
In all its new-wrought robes of freshest hue
    Surveyed the glorious landscape, spread below
A sky that seemed another sea of blue
    Upreared on pillars capitaled with snow.
But, O how swelled his heart when solemn night
    With light and silence flooded all the scene,
And bathed in glist'ning beauty, marble height,
    Meand'ring rill and forest wall of green ;
While overhead, the world of blue was hung
    With new-created stars, that seemed to be
In love with all the charms of earth, and flung
    Their radiant splendors on the slumb'ring sea.

O what a joy it was at such an hour,
    When earth was young and fair as heav'n above,
To stray with Venus to some vernal bow'r,
    And feel that all the new-born world was love ;
To see the naiad from some shadowed stream
    Emerge and backward brush her dripping hair,

Then stand amazed, as waking from a dream,
  To find herself and all the world so fair;
At early dawn in chaste Diana's train
  To roam abroad across the breezy hills;
To hear Apollo wake on earth the strain
  That gods in golden hall with rapture thrills;
To see the swift-winged herald earthward sweep
  And let some newly given blessing fall
From radiant lip, yet dyed with purple deep
  Of nectar, lately quaffed in heav'nly hall;
In grove of shimm'ring streams and hallowed shades
  To meet Minerva, fair of brow, and stray
Where leafy arches crown the colonnades,
  And feel the bosom swell beneath the sway
Of glowing thoughts expressed in tones that wove
  Together liquid murmuring of the rill,
The mystic lispings of the leafy grove,
  Its sense of holy calmness, hushed and still.

And thus they taught his ear to love each sound
  Of harmony that stirs the human soul.
He stood enrapt, as on enchanted ground,
  And thrills ecstatic through his being stole,
When sang the nightingale in distant glen,
  Or swaying boughs in sweetest whispers bore

Their welcome to the wanton wind, or when
  The Triton blew his shell upon the shore.

To love all forms of beauty he had learned,
  Beneath their kindly guidance and control.
To this his eyes they constantly had turned
  Till beauty grew the passion of his soul.
A rose that slept with slightly parted lips
  And breathed its fragrance to the airs of night ;
A pine that stretched its dainty finger-tips
  To grasp the glories of the world of light ;
A naiad standing on a lakelet beach
  With swelling breast of snow and beaming brow,
Uplifting high her shapely arm to reach
  An op'ning bud on overhanging bough,
Would make him pause and tremble as a maid
  Before a shrine : into his eyes there came
The glint of tears, around his lips there played
  A smile, and tremors ran through all his frame.

Minerva, too, had taught his hand to mould
  In marble pure whatever form he chose ;
He deftly shaped the roses, fold in fold,
  And drooping lilies, wrapped in all their snows.

The nymph that paused and raised her slender hand
　To list'ning ear to catch a distant sound,
In eager expectation there would stand
　With all her charms in marble fetters bound.

But though in realms of beauty he abode,
　Though nymph and naiad haunted grove and
　　stream,
Though gods were his companions, and bestowed
　Whate'er would satisfy his wildest dream,
Yet still (perchance by gods themselves inspired),
　There grew a yearning, vague and undefined,
For what his lonely heart had long desired,—
　Communion with a creature of his kind.

On this he mused, until at last he burned
　In marble an ideal form to mould.
The symmetry he in himself discerned,
　Whatever charm in nymph he could behold,
Whatever beauty loving Venus bore,
　Whatever grace Diana's form displayed,
The brow of wisdom calm Minerva wore,
　Should, all combined, be in this form portrayed.

He found a block of marble, pure and white
   As when the busy hand of winter sifts
Its rarest down, and wand'ring winds of night
   Heap all in flowing curves and billowy drifts.
His dream of perfect beauty here he shaped
   To lines of grace, with loving hand and warm,
In folds of drifted snow enrobed and draped,
   That half concealed yet still revealed its form.
But O, how did his pulses leap and bound
   When thus complete he saw the figure stand ;
The shapely arm, that tapered true and round
   To slender wrist with dainty lily hand ;
The bosom, that a moment seemed to rest
   When risen to its highest, fullest swell,
Where falling robe revealed the downy nest
   Where all the Loves and Graces chose to dwell,—
Where, pillowed, one forever might repose,
   Forget all pleasure of the earth in this,
For rapture, nevermore his eyelids close,
   Or, dream away his happy life in bliss ;
The shapely head, on shining shoulders set
   That rose in glossy whiteness full and round,
As when the winter's playful winds have met
   And heaped in swelling curves a snowy mound ;
The brow, that in serenest calmness beamed

With light of loving heart and gifted mind ;
The hair, that framed the forehead round, and
    streamed
In wealth of waving tresses unconfined ;
The eyes, that looked a truth and tenderness
    That into all the heart's recesses stole,
Yet seemed a light of wisdom to possess
    That burst from chambers of the inmost soul ;
Thin lips, of dainty curve and parting slight
    Like op'ning petals of the earliest bloom,
Whence kindly words, e'er waiting for their flight,
    Would float, soft-winged and sweet as faint per-
    fume,—
The lips, where smiles of loving tenderness
    So frequent had allowed their sweets to lie
That it were earthly bliss enough to press
    Those lips but once, then swoon for joy and die.

This marble form was now his only thought,
    Forgot were all the beauties of his home,
The company of gods no more he sought,
    And at their side no longer would he roam.
It stood within the shadow of a grove,
    Where pines of rarest green embow'red it round,

Where passing clouds their fleeting shadows wove
  And distant rill sang low with dreamy sound.
Day ever found him kneeling at the shrine;
  When Night her glad but silent glances threw
And lit the form with splendor more divine,
  His burning heart no bounds of rapture knew.

Thus constantly before it would he stand,
  His heart aflame, his lips entranced and dumb;
He often thought she beckoned with her hand,
  Unsealed her lips and softly whispered, "Come!"
At last, he made his yearning heart believe,
  (Since gods had ne'er his wildest wish denied,)
This might perchance the breath of life receive,
  And as companion wander at his side.

While morning flushed the east with tints of flame,
  Within the grove where earnestly he prayed
Minerva fair and radiant Venus came
  And stood beside the figure he had made.
Their presence to the scene a glory lent;
  They smiled and listened to his pleading prayer;
Each as her head she bowed to give assent,
  A finger laid upon the marble there.

A thrill, a flush through all the figure ran,
    But cheek and lip were tinged with deeper dyes ;
To sink and swell the snowy breast began,
    And light and life to sparkle in the eyes.
She saw him there, she bent her graceful head,
    Her cheek was flushed with yet a deeper flame,
A smile ineffable her lips o'erspread,
    Then, gliding down, with open arms she came.
He fondly clasped her to a throbbing breast
    That all its wildest ecstasy revealed ;
The snowy brow, the crimsoned cheek he pressed,
    The silence of the fragrant lips unsealed.

Then o'er the hills the rosy morning streamed,
    And on the grove a flame of splendor flung,
In brighter beauty radiant Venus beamed,
    And on Minerva's brow a glory hung.
The goddesses, ascending, passed away
    To heaven's golden halls, and left alone
The happy pair, where'er they pleased to stray ;
    Before them lay the world, and all their own.

He took her by the dainty lily hand
    And in the gold of morning left the bow'r.

He found a rarer beauty in the land,
  A fresher fragrance in the budding flow'r.
And, list'ning to the music of her words,
  That thrilled him with their low and varied tones,
Perceived a richer note in voice of birds,
  Or streamlet murm'ring over mossy stones.
The gods were dearer to him than before,
  With richer hand their blessings they bestowed ;
To roam by stream or on the sounding shore,
  Descended oftener from their high abode.
They frequent came the youthful pair to meet ;
  By noble thought awoke the earnest mind ;
By charming sound or sight, and odor sweet,
  Infused the soul with pleasure more refined.
A newer light of splendor o'er the grove,
  A richer verdure over plain and hill,
On rose a rarer tint, they cast, and strove
  Their happy life to make yet happier still.

His dream of perfect bliss was thus fulfilled,
  His happy choice in love and wisdom made.
By day, the fruitful earth they dressed and tilled,
  At evening rested in its hallowed shade.

In her he found the love for which he yearned,
  A finer sense, a deeper feeling shown ;
In all their happy converse he discerned
  A heart that beat responsive to his own.
And thus the gladsome days went gliding by
  In lands of sunny sky and scented airs ;
The gods above no blessing would deny,
  Nor earth below, for all the earth was theirs.

Morton Hall.

NEAR the storm-swept sea there's a tranquil bay,
  Rock-bastioned by Nature's hand ;
At its inlet small in their robes of gray
  Two guardian rock-cliffs stand.
And so near they stand that can scarcely glide
  The boat on the wave between ;
The sun's bright rays never light its tide
  Nor stars find a glass serene.
On the sea without may the Tempest rave
  Till stream back his hoary locks,
And his steed spur on through the foamy waves
  To charge the unyielding rocks ;
But the bay within is asleep the while,
  And scarce heaves the slumb'ring breast,
The storm without only makes it smile,
  But never can mar its rest.

By this tranquil bay is a village neat,
  And here, in the summer, they
Who are seeking rest in some cool retreat,
  From the noise of the city stray.
  3

There was one friend there, with a pale, sweet face,
　　In days of the long ago,
Who had made her home in the quiet place,
　　Unmindful of winter snow.
When the winter came 'twas a wild, weird home,
　　But she loved it not the less ;
She had beauty found in its frozen foam,
　　And charms in its loneliness.
For a maiden strange was this Florence More,
　　Her history none could tell,
Since she never spoke of her life before
　　She came by this bay to dwell.
When we asked the maid of this time to speak,
　　We wished all our words unsaid,
Such a pallor rose on the maiden's cheek,
　　Such dimness her eyes o'erspread.
All the past to her seemed a close-sealed book,
　　Enwritten with bitter tears,
On whose pages she never dared to look
　　And read of the bygone years.

By her gentle ways she had cheered the heart
　　Of all who the place had known,
And yet each well knew that some hidden dart
　　Was piercing the while her own.

For though often smiles round her lip would play,
　They ever would die again,
As the glad harp-song when the hand will stray
　And waken a mournful strain.
Yet the dear pale face when it came brought light,
　New charms to each circle gave,
As when moonbeams break from a cloud at night
　And silver the rippling wave.

In the days gone by, with this Florence More
　I loved in the eve to stray
Where the clear waves tripped on the sandy shore
　That circled around the bay.
As we walked one eve, " Look you there," she said,
　" How waves and their restless sands
All the footprints made on their smooth-worn bed
　Efface with their busy hands !
Oh ! I wish the paths of the bitter past,
　Where prints of my feet remain,
Were thus smoothed, to be but a blank at last,
　Or all trodden o'er again."
" Let the past," I cried, " be a past forgot ;
　'Twill then seem a blank once more.
Let the gloomy clouds of the past come not
　To darken the way before.

Do not think that thine is the only heart
   That throbs in the human breast
And, the while, is pierced with a cruel dart,
   And finds from its pain no rest.
There is not a heart, though it lightly beat,
   But treasures *some* grief untold
Which it never dares to the world repeat—
   A world that it deems too cold.
Oh ! those heart-hid pains would, half-told, disclose
   More grief than the world has known.
What the human heart can reveal none knows
   Until he has searched his own."

" Not a truer word could thy lips repeat,"
   A voice at our side exclaimed
As we passed a rock but to reach whose feet
   The waves ever vainly aimed.
We a stranger found as we quickly turned
   The speaker of this to seek ;
In his eye the glow of his youth still burned,
   And fled not his sun-browned cheek.
" On the shelving rock pray you take a seat,"
   He said, and forsook his own,
" And a tale will I of my life repeat
   That never the world has known."

With his eyes bent low on the smooth-worn sand,
  As if he could there behold
All his life outspread by some mystic hand,
  The stranger his story told :

" On Old England's shore where the wild waves hide
  The rocks, with their tresses white,
'Mid a shady grove, on a manor wide
  Arises a Hall in sight.
On this manor broad, in a clump of trees,
  The home of my youth is seen
Where first the breath of the coming breeze
  Sets moving the leaflets green.
For my home was not in this Morton Hall ;
  With humbler was I content,
As a rector's son ; for the Mortons all
  Could boast of their long descent.

" In the years gone by, to this mansion grand
  A messenger came one day,
And the door flung wide with his icy hand
  And beckoned the sire away.
But he heeded not how the father yearned
  To gaze on the dear young face

Of his only child, as away he turned,
 Or clasp her in fond embrace.

" With this little Stell I in childhood played ;
 We built in the grove our home ;
By the splashing rills we together strayed
 And laughed at their spray and foam.
Through the Childhood Land we thus made our
  way ;
 We gathered the sweetest flow'rs
On the sunny banks of the streamlets gay,
 And joy winged the fleeting hours.

" While we lingered still in this Childhood Land,
 Though now were the bounds in view,
To the Hall again came the icy hand
 And beckoned the mother too.
Then in bright-lipped Stell we a change could trace—
 More womanly grew her ways ;
But there lingered still in her woman's grace
 The sweetness of childhood days.
And the change in her wrought in me a change—
 Less boyish my bearing grew.
In our altered life found we pleasure strange,
 And charms in employments new.

" But the time drew near, as on wings of gold
    Years fled in their flight away,
When in Learning's halls, 'mid their treasures old,
    My feet for a time must stray.
Soon the hour came when we for years must part,
    Whose moments would slowly fly ;
But we vowed we still would be one in heart
    In mem'ry of days gone by ;
And I wore a pledge of the maiden's truth
    To cheer me in future strife—
Is it strange that we who had walked through youth
    Should dream of a walk through life ?

" Ere I went, my sire, who our secret guessed
    But lent not approving eye,
Bade me cherish not in my youthful breast
    This dream of the days gone by.
' In the past, with joy, you have side by side
    Been walking life's way,' he said,
' But in future years will be sundered wide
    The paths that you each must tread.
Hand in hand you've walked, but know not how Gold
    And Pride, with relentless hands,
Can dissever hearts that in days of old
    Were linked by the closest bands.

To the maiden's shrine will the rich and gay
　　In days of the future flee,
And the poor young friend of her childhood play
　　Quite soon will forgotten be.'
'True, the maid,' I cried, 'has what heart can crave,
　　Has gold and has widespread lands,
While the wealth have I that the good God gave—
　　A brain and two willing hands.
But a love yet stronger than love of gold
　　God plants in the hearts of youth ;
And he gave her wealth of a price untold—
　　He gave her a *heart of truth.*'

" So away I sped, and but slowly passed
　　The years in their weary round ;
But arrived the hour of return at last,
　　And home I again was found.
How each well-known scene where my youth was
　　　　spent
　　Brought back its enjoyments all !
I not long delayed ere my steps I bent
　　To visit old Morton Hall.
O'er earth had Night just her mantle flung,
　　And, bent o'er its heaving breast,

She the sweetest song of the zephyr sung,
  To hush it to perfect rest.
And upon the floor of the tree-arched aisle
  She carpets of dapple threw,
While the stars on high with a cheery smile
  Looked down from their homes of blue.
Then the moon arose from her couch of snow
  And flung back the curtain light,
And bending out with her brow aglow,
  Looked down on the starry night ;
While words of cheer did each passing breeze
  In whispers to me repeat,
And with beck'ning hand stood the list'ning trees
  To hasten my ling'ring feet.

" Lightly beat my heart as I onward went,
  And soon was the Hall in sight ;
'Gainst the columned porch, as a statue, leant
  Fair Stell in her garments white.
From her brow the breeze brushed her tresses brown,
  Her cheeks with its pure breath fanned,
And the climbing vine had but now dropped down
  A rose in her open hand.

" As I deemed that she for my coming stayed,
    A youth, from a column nigh,
Sprang upon his steed, all in gold arrayed,
    And waved her a kind good-bye.
But some icy hand seemed to me to fall
    Just then on my heart of fire,
For then suddenly were remembered all
    The words of my warning sire.
' Is it thus,' I said in reproving tones,
    ' That you for my coming wait ?'
She replied, ' May not, when one mate is flown,
    The bird seek another mate ?'
' Then thy vows of truth were all false,' I cried,
    And turned from the maiden's sight,
And I flung aside in my angry pride
    The hand that had checked my flight ;
For my heart was proud, and my wounded pride,
    As rocks, would no yielding know,
Which spurn again the insulting tide
    Though robed in a jewelled snow.

" As I fled, the moon, as she sad gazed down,
    A glance of reproval threw,
And the stars on high with an angry frown
    Looked down from their homes of blue.

Their reproaching words did each passing breeze
　　In hisses to me repeat,
While with pointing hands stood the taunting trees
　　To call back my hast'ning feet.

" But I heeded not as away I sped,
　　Nor knew where I made my way ;
But at last the madd'ning impulse led
　　My feet where a vessel lay.
I ne'er stayed my steps nor a glance cast round ;
　　I gave not a thought, but sprung
To the vessel's deck with a sudden bound
　　As she from her mooring swung.
'Twas a wild, rash act of my wounded pride,
　　Repented with bitter tears,
In a *moment's* rage thus to cast aside
　　The true-hearted friend of *years.*

" It was long ere I could again return ;
　　And e'en when I came unknown
To my native land, it was but to learn
　　The maid from her home had flown.
And a tale is whispered at Morton Hall
　　That she, when her loved one came,

Had some idle words from her lip let fall
  That wounded his heart of flame.
He had fled her sight in his rage and grief,
  And she, in her heart-deep woe,
From the Hall had fled to obtain relief,
  But whither did no one know.
But they darkly point to a rocky steep
  Where garment of hers was found,
Where, to end her grief, in the surging deep
  She madly had leaped and drowned.
Oh ! my heart's last drop would I give to know
  That she who sleeps 'neath that wave,
To the cruel wretch who had wronged her so
  One glance of forgiveness gave."

Then with trembling feet uprose Florence More,
  These words from her pale lip fell :
"I have pardoned thee, Lawrence, o'er and o'er,
  But hast thou forgiven Stell ? "
And with quiv'ring lip she then told him all—
  That here she had changed her name ;
That her nurse alone at old Morton Hall
  Had known that she hither came ;

That the garment found on the rocky steep
  Forgotten had been one day
When from scenes recalling her sorrow deep
  She fled to the shore away.

I arose and stole from the quiet place,
  But they tarried on the shore.
When I saw them next, still, methought, each face
  A *shadow* of sorrow wore ;
But upon each, too, there was such a smile
  As earth in the spring puts on
When the flow'rs appear and the birds the while
  Announce the drear winter gone.

A Day with Homer.

METHOUGHT the stream of Time had backward rolled,
And I was standing on the fruitful plain
That lay between the sea and ancient Troy.
I saw one standing on the curving beach,
Whose hoary locks were playthings for the wind
That fresh'ning came across the swelling waves.
I listened to the mystic music of a voice
That chanted to their measured beat, in tones
Now whispering soft and low as rustling leaves,
Now rolling with the boom of tumbling waves,
Now clanging as the clash of brazen arms.

He waved his magic hand.   Aurora fair,
Arising from her loved Tithonus' side,
With rosy fingers deftly backward drew
The crimson curtains of the ruddy dawn
And ushered in the day.   Afar appeared
A mighty fleet, whose dark and curving prows
Were cleaving fast the tossing waves, impelled
By oars that lashed the sea to hoary foam,

Or sails that forward bent their snowy breasts
In eager haste to reach the sounding shore.

Again the minstrel waved his magic hand.
Upon the yielding beach updrawn, the ships
Lay propped.   Unnumbered hosts upon the shore
Were marshalled.   Mighty kings with gleaming helms
Of nodding plume, and fourfold shields that shone
As noonday suns, and tow'ring ashen spears
With glitt'ring points of ruthless piercing bronze.
To curving chariot yoked, the shapely steeds
Whose ample manes, down-flowing, swept the ground,
Impatient stood, swift-footed as the blast.

Outstreaming from the Scæan gates of Troy
There issued forth a host in like array.
Then with a shout that shook the archèd sky
These hosts advancing, met upon the plain.
Bows twanged and bitter arrows winged their way
To gallant breasts, and dyed the ivory skin
With purple stain.   Huge glitt'ring spears, impelled
By mighty arms, resounding rang on shields ;
Or, piercing, cleft both shield and glancing helm
Of brass, and hurled the hero crashing down

Upon the earth, with loud-resounding arms,
And spread a veil of darkness o'er his eyes.
Fleet-footed steeds, with manes back-streaming, flew
Across the plain with whirling chariot bright,
Whose drivers urged them on with stinging lash
To bear the crested warrior to the fray ;
Or, prince and driver gone, the car o'erturned,
With panting nostril, wild, distended eyes,
They plunged in mad confusion through the host.

He waved his hand.   Afar across the sea
I saw divine Olympus lifting high
Its form sublime, and on a marble base
Of snow upreared, with dome of blue above,
The glorious palace of the heav'nly gods.
They in their golden halls, with purple lip
Were quaffing nectar sweet that Hebe fair
Presented each in gleaming cups of gold.
They sat upon their lofty shining thrones,
And feasted on ambrosia rich, and heard
The harp, whose golden strings Apollo swept
Till breasts were thrilled and melted with the strains
That spread like fragrance through the vaulted hall.

Supreme on shining throne, in splendor sat
Majestic Jove, whose nod imperious shook
Olympus to its base, but yet who feared
The stinging taunts of jealous Juno's tongue.
Deceiving with her craft immortal Jove,
But shrinking when his anger was aroused,
Yet yielding not the purpose of her heart,
On lofty couch of gold resplendent sat
Imperial Juno, stately queen, of large
And lustrous eye, and shapely snowy arm,
And fragrant bosom dear to mighty Jove.

Beside her sat Minerva, fair of brow,
Alert to prompt with wingèd thought her queen ;
And he of skilful hand but limping feet,
Who wrought in gold the chambers of the gods.
Arrayed in panoply of jangling brass,
There, too, sat cruel-eyed, broad-shouldered Mars,
Who wore the fiercest brow of all the gods.

There sat the virgin queen whose buskined feet
Are swift to chase at early dawn, across
The breezy hills, the flying stag that falls
By wingèd shaft shot from her sounding bow ;

4

And Venus, favored child of mighty Jove,
With perfect moulded arm and breast of snow,
Mirth-lighted eye and soft caressing hand ;—
Love, fairest form that ever found a home
On earth, or in the golden halls of heaven.

Thus there were gathered all the immortal ones
Who meet at Jove's command in heavenly hall.
Although endowed with human hates and loves,
Yet all were gods, and godlike seemed they all.
Sublimity celestial clothed their brows
And wrapped their forms in more than mortal
    grace.

He waved his hand.   Obedient to the call,
Then mighty Jove arose and swiftly yoked
His brazen-footed, golden-manèd steeds
To brazen chariot bright, and grasping fast
The golden reins, came sweeping down
The shining slopes of his Olympic home,
And swifter than his lightning, shot athwart
The sky, and sat, in gleaming gold arrayed,
Upon the heights of Ida, many-rilled.

I saw the heav'nly portals open wide.
Upon a silver car with golden wheels
Imperial Juno rode, and at her side
Minerva, clad in panoply of war.
The queen of heav'n with outstretched, radiant arms
Held firm the shining reins, until her steeds
With glitt'ring feet far-reaching, measured swift
The airy space across the purple sky
And bore her down upon the plains of Troy.

Then Neptune, too, forsook the wooded height
Of Samos, and came swiftly striding down ;
And ent'ring, neath the sea, his home
Of gold and crystal, quickly yoked
His tawny-manèd steeds.   Across the deep to Troy
He sped in glitt'ring car, whose whirling wheels
Cleft through the parting waves a level way ;
While round the car the creatures of his realm
Careered, rejoicing at the presence of their king.

Thus came the gods to mingle in the fray
With men upon the plains of Troy.   I saw
Dread Diomedes wound with wanton spear
The clinging arm that loving Venus drew

About her son to save him from his foe.
I heard her piteous wail, and saw the drops
That dyed the clasping arm with crimson stain.
I saw him pierce, with brazen point, the side
Of Mars, and heard the god when wild with pain
He roared as loud as many thousand men.
Again I saw the vengeful god, when mad
He rushed against Minerva, azure-eyed,
And smote her fringèd ægis with his spear.
But swift she hurled him crashing down.
He covered acres wide.   His streaming locks
And brazen arms were all defiled in dust.

I saw Achilles, unexcelled in strength,
In manly beauty unsurpassed, by all
The princely Greeks who fought on Trojan field.
A king that by deliberate choice preferred
A short but glorious career, to long
And peaceful reign among his Myrmidons.
A king whose every act was passion-swayed
By love of fame or friend, or fierce revenge.
His thoughts were not concealed with cunning craft,
But swift escaped the barriers of his teeth.

When Agamemnon swore with angry threat
To rob him of Briseis, fair-cheeked bride,
I saw his mighty frame convulse with rage,
His fingers clutch and half unsheathe his sword ;
While taunts and bold reproaches rained from lip
That hotly hurled the hated insult back.
And when they led the unwilling maid away,
I saw the tear that stained his rugged cheek
As lone he sat upon the sobbing shore,
And called his goddess mother from the deep,
Unbosomed all the burden of his heart
And prayed for vengeance from the heavenly gods.

When Agamemnon sent imploring aid
And vowed the maid uninjured to restore,
I saw him spurn in proud disdain the bribe
Of Lesbian maids, and steeds of tossing mane,
And hand of princess rich, whose father deemed
A wounded spirit could be cured by gold.

When dearest friend had fallen in the fray,
I saw him lowly bow his head, and heap
The ashes on his comely locks, and lie

Prostrated on the shore, while sobs betrayed
The grief that lay so heavy on his heart.

I saw him don the greaves, the corselet bright,
The helm of golden crest, the wondrous shield,
That Vulcan wrought.   I saw him grasp his spear
Of Pelian ash, and mount his stately car.
I saw the steed, caparisoned in gold,
That bowed its graceful yellow-manèd neck
And warned its master of his coming fate.

I heard his loud exultant shout that sent
A thrill of fear through all the Trojan host.
I saw him raging wreak a fierce revenge
For dear Patroclus' death.   He reveled in his
    wrath,
And slaughtered Trojan foes, till all the earth
And all his beauteous arms were black with gore.
He spared nor prince nor peasant in his path,
Nor even spared the unarmed fugitive
Who knelt and begged for mercy at his feet.

There Hector, too, I saw, in gleaming arms,
Alert and active in defence of Troy.

He fought not for revenge or fame, but home
And kindred, loving wife and infant child.

I saw him pass the Scæan gates, when back
Again he turned the fleeing hosts, then stride
Away to Priam's palace high, to bid,
In tones of reverence and filial love,
His aged mother to the goddess pray,
And offer garment rich with wondrous work,
Lest dread destruction might upon them fall.

I saw him meet white-armed Andromache,
His tall and graceful wife, the fairest dame
Of all that wore the trailing Trojan robe.
When weeping, clinging to his hand, she told
How father, mother, brothers, all, were slain,
And how she feared for him, her all in all;
I saw the hero bend his crested head
And soothe with gentle hand his weeping wife.
I heard his tender tones as low he spoke
Of sacred Troy in ruins; brothers brave
And aged Priam trampled in its dust;
Of all the hidden pain that rent his heart
When he remembered some harsh-minded Greek

Would lead away his tender bride, a slave,
To weave the web with tears, and water bear,
In Argos, for some haughty Grecian dame.
But yet his heart must falter not nor fear,
And he must do his task, as she her own,
And patient wait the stern decrees of fate.

And then he reached his hand to clasp his child ;
But when it shrieked to see the nodding crest,
He laid his glittering helmet down and took
The fearful babe caressing to his arms,
And, having prayed a blessing from the gods,
Restored him to his mother's yearning breast
As she stood smiling through her recent tears.
A hero he that found 'mid din of arms
A tender word for mother, wife and child.

I saw him yoke to chariot of war
His wind-swift steeds, and send the hostile Greeks
In tumult flocking back across the plain,
Then burst exultant through their vaunted walls
And scatter flames among the updrawn prows.
His glancing helm was ever first of all ;
His form the foremost in the thickest fray.

Again I saw him as he stood alone
Without the walls of Troy, when all had fled
And left their brave defender to his fate,
Resolved to face the dreaded foe and win,
Or die a not inglorious death. He hurled
His spear with mighty force and truest aim,
But harmlessly it fell upon the shield
That skilful Vulcan wrought in heaven's forge.
Then, though he knew his fated hour was nigh,
Undaunted still, he drew his gleaming blade
And rushed upon his god-assisted foe.
I saw Achilles pierce with ruthless spear
His tender neck. I saw his princely form
And proudly nodding plume prostrated low ;
I saw the iron-hearted victor o'er
His fate exult, deny his dying prayer,
And strip his shoulders of their shining arms.
Then thrusting through his feet the cruel thongs,
He bound him to his brazen car, and trailed
His noble head and streaming locks behind.

I heard the wails of woe on Trojan walls,
Saw aged Priam, in his deep despair,
Lie groaning on the ground. I heard the shriek,

The piteous cries and moans of Hecuba.
I saw her cast her shining head-dress by
And wildly rend her streaming silver hair,
As she beheld her bravest son, her boast,
The darling of her heart and lofty Troy,
Thus dead and dragged in dark defiling dust.

I saw Andromache among her maids,
And they were weaving work of wondrous art ;
But, thoughtful of her Hector's swift return,
Had warmed a bath to soothe his wearied limbs.
She heard the shriek of aged Hecuba,
And fearing for her dearest, rushed away,
Like one distracted, to the tower wall.
She saw the sight.   Then strength forsook her limbs,
And sense her soul.   Upon the earth she sank,
And from her head the veil and fillet fell,
Revealing all the glory of the brow
And marble breast that gallant Hector loved.
I saw the streaming tears of Trojan dames
As low they bent about her shapely form.
I saw her faintly rise and wring her hands,
 While sighs and sobs her swelling bosom shook.
I heard her low and pitiful lament ;—

Her faithful husband fallen in his youth,
Defence of her and all the Trojan dames ;
The insult heaped upon the harmless head
Of Hector's infant son, that oft had sat
And richly fed, upon his father's knee ;
The dying hand her fingers had not clasped ;
The faltering lips that left no loving word
To be remembered all her life with tears.

Once more the minstrel waved his magic hand.
The golden sun sank in the ocean down,
And darkness slowly fell.   The fruitful plain,
The gods and heroes vanished from my sight.
But still, across the centuries of years,
I hear the mystic music of that voice,
I see the glories of that wondrous scene.

An Autumn Day.

THE clouds in sombre garments were arrayed,
    And seemed as silent mourners bending low
To watch the earth's last trace of beauty fade
    Before they robed it in its shroud of snow.

The very winds were hushed, as if for fear
    They might bewail the dying earth ere dead;
But gloomy Night seemed ever hov'ring near,
    As if in haste the dark'ning pall to spread.

The autumn glories knew the rider, Death,
    Among them came by night on courser pale;
They saw his footprints, found his frozen breath
    At morn, beside the stream and o'er the vale.

With cruel hand he smote the grove-clad hill
    And left the tender leaflets wounded sore;
Some clinging to their parents, bleeding still,
    Some fallen, dead and darkened with their gore.

And Nature's children prized their wealth no more
  When near the dread, unpitying courser drew;
The tiny vine exposed its ample store
  Of purple clusters openly to view;

The orchard with its hands low reaching down,
  Its golden hoardings offered free to all;
The forest tree unclasped from treasure brown
  The fingers wide and let it idly fall;

The richly mantled cedar and the pine
  Alone had skill his onset to withstand,
And, sheltered at their feet, the nestling vine
  And fairy-broidered fern escaped his hand.

Earth's lovely flower-children all were dead,
  Or drooping low to life they feebly clung,
Save where some new-born beauty reared its head,
  That Death had thought too fair to die so young.

Though dimmed was earth's bright summer-robe of
    green,
  As to the grove I strayed that autumn day,
Though deep'ning gloom pervaded all the scene,
  No weight of sadness on *my* bosom lay.

I well remembered how had passed away
   Glad-hearted Spring and gentle Summer fair ;
I knew that Death would soon beside them lay
   Loved, dreamy Autumn with her golden hair ;

I knew that Winter's swift-advancing feet
   Would soon among earth's prostrate beauties tread ;
His chilly hand would soon in winding sheet
   Enwrap alike the dying and the dead ;

I knew earth would be drear with cold and gloom
   When these would all in sleep of death recline,
Yet in my bosom sadness found no room,
   And on that day a cheerful heart was mine.

A heart that whispered, " Winter passes too,
   Glad-hearted Spring will wake again and rise,
Fair Summer come with all her charms anew,
   And dreamy Autumn with her hazel eyes ;

Nor on earth's breast her children shall lie dead,
   But Spring shall come and kiss the damp of death
From each cold brow, and raise the drooping head,
   And fill the lifeless lips with quick'ning breath.

A heart that shall, I trust, through life be mine ;
  That shall, though Spring and Summer sink to rest,
Though Autumn, too, to Winter shall resign,
  From every trace of sadness keep my breast.

A heart that even when I sink at last
  My sleep upon the breast of earth to take,
Shall say, "This winter, too, shall soon be past,
  And Spring eternal shall thy slumbers break."

The Sculptors.

WE all are sculptors in this world of ours,
   There's not a hand but may some image form
That, when the Master comes to view our task,
   Shall from his lip receive approval warm.

The images are carved from rocks of gray,
   From marble stained with frequent dusky bands;
They, too, are carved from marble pure and white
   As Paro's breast when bared by Grecian hands.

One from a faultless block of spotless snow
   Will shape a queenly form of perfect mould,
That breathless seems to wait till Life shall place
   Within its hands her flick'ring lamp to hold.

Another idly leaves the task undone,
   With here and there perchance a finished part
That shows how beauteous might have been the form
   Completed, had the hand but used its art.

Some, aimless, chip the precious block away ;
   Or strive to shape some phantom of the brain,
Forever altering its fleeting form,
   Till only fragments of the block remain.

And some, with block of marble rough and stained,
   Will skilfully avoid the dusky bands ;
And none would ever know that such had been,
   So fair an image issues from their hands.

And some with but the gray and stubborn rock,
   Will, still undaunted, labor patiently
Until rewards their persevering toil
   A stately form of perfect symmetry.

And some, because they have but rock of gray,
   Or marble soiled with frequent dusky stain,
And not a block as pure as winter snow,
   Will fling aside the chisel in disdain.

While *this* one, blust'ring, toiled at some design,
   The world approved and thought its praises just ;
But, when it came to view the work complete,
   It found some hideous form or naught but dust.

   5

While *that* was patient bending o'er his task,
   The world had scoffed ; but, as again it turned
When long the artist had been gone, it found
   A grandeur that it ne'er before discerned.

And *here,* one carved perchance a tiny flow'r,
   Whereon the world ne'er deigned to bend its gaze :
But rarest beauty here the Master found,
   And here bestowed His warmest words of praise.

We all are sculptors in this world of ours ;
   There's not a hand but may some image form,
That, when the Master comes to view our task,
   Shall from His lip receive approval warm.

If, when the Master comes, He find
   The block untouched, the form left incomplete,
But dust and fragments or some hideous shape,
   Alas, how shall we then that Master meet ?

The Seven Ages of Woman.

A BABE, that nestles in its mother's arms
   And prattles e'er of fairy Babyland ;
A tripping school-girl, bright with budding charms ;
   A maiden queen, that rules with loving hand ;
A bride, with brow touched half by joy and fear ;
   A mother, 'mid her flock with cheek aglow ;
A gray-haired dame, that sheds the ready tear
   O'er vanished scenes and friends of long ago ;
A tott'ring form, that walks through Childhood lands,
   Sees not their beauties, thrills not with their mirth,
That wearies on the way, and folds the hands
   And nestles in the mother arms of earth.

The Human Heart.

WHAT sunny hope, what dark despair,
What happiness, what gnawing care,
What innocence, what sin,
   That treasure-house,
   That prison-house,
   The human heart,
May hold within!

The Young Mother.

"I shall go to him, but he shall not return to me."

WHILE Spring the land with lavish hand
   Bedecked with leaf and blossom,
She near me strayed, and gently laid
   A flow'ret in my bosom;

But Autumn came, with sword and flame
   The forest leaflet blasting,
And bud and bloom without a tomb
   On Earth's cold bosom casting.

And oh, *my* flow'r, that happy hour
  To me in love had given,
His cruel grasp, from clinging clasp
  And bleeding breast, had riven.

The bird that flies to other skies
  When summer days are over,
Will come when Spring abroad shall fling
  Her flag of fragrant clover;

The forest tree the blast may see
  Its robe in tatters rending,
But robe as fair the tree shall wear
  When wintry days are ending;

But bird may come and tree may bloom,
  As Spring shall bid them ever;
Alas, for me, my eye shall see
  My babe returning never.

The Child's Call.

"Mother, in the lowly bed
  Where thy darling they have laid,
    Lone I am, so lone.
  Though the blossoms at my head
  Never are allowed to fade,
  Daily by thy hand renewed,
  Fragrant-scented, brilliant-hued,
    Lone I am, so lone.

"Though around me as I sleep
  Grass is waving cool and deep,
    Lone I am, so lone.
  Night-winds whisper as they pass
  Lulling sounds among the grass,
  But, dear mother, still I long
  For thy soothing cradle song,—
    Lone I am, so lone.

"Though the stars up in the sky
  Shine upon me where I lie,
    Lone I am, so lone.

Here I need thy presence still,
For my chamber's dark and chill ;
Come, dear mother, come and keep
Close beside me while I sleep,
    Lone I am, so lone.

" Dearest mother, here I miss
Clasping arm and good-night kiss,
    Cold I am, so cold.
Mother, here I cannot rest,
Let me nestle in thy breast ;
Mother, fold about my form
Loving arms to keep me warm,
    Cold I am, so cold."

Thus the mother heard her child
Calling 'mid the tempest wild,—
Calling as she toiled by day,
Calling when she sleepless lay,—
And the moon was shining bright
In the silence of the night ;
Even when she slept, the same
Pleading voice in whispers came,
Ever in that plaintive tone,
" Mother, I am cold and lone."

So the mother rose at last,
To the restless sleeper passed,
Softly down beside her lay,
Never left her night or day.
There together now they sleep
In their narrow chamber deep;
There the baby lies at rest,
Folded to the mother's breast.
Ever on their lowly bed
Sweetest blooms their fragrance shed;
Stars above them in the sky
Shine upon them where they lie;
Night-winds whisper as they pass
Lulling sounds among the grass.
There no more, as calm they sleep,
Aught shall mar their slumber deep,
Nevermore the plaintive tone,
"Mother, I am cold and lone."

Early Blighted.

As OFT we see some op'ning flow'er-gem,
　　Though watched and tended, droop and fade away,
Nor know the reason till the fallen stem
　　Reveals the place where the destroyer lay ;
So we saw every trace of bloom depart,
　　We saw her slender frame was wasting fast,
Nor knew the weight of sorrow at her heart
　　That snapped in twain the thread of life at last.

　　Pallid face so lily white,
　　Wavy tresses, amber bright,
　　Backward brushed from forehead pale ;
　　Lying still with eyelids closed
　　As if she in dreamland vale
　　After weary toil reposed.
　　Lips together closely pressed
　　As if she in broken rest
　　Fearful was she might impart
　　Hidden secret of the heart.

Hands, that on the bosom lie
As if any rising sigh,
Any swelling sigh of pain,
Any sigh of restlessness,
Any heaving, they would fain
With their folding clasp suppress.
Silent does the sleeper rest
As a leaflet on the breast
Of some stilly lakelet laid
Where no breezes dare invade.

Friends with silent movement glide
To the sleeping maiden's side:
Some are there whom hand of age
Hath encrowned with silver hair,
Some whose brows are but a page
Written by the pen of care.
Sad they are o'er one so young
Death his mantle dark had flung,
O'er a fair and tender bud
Bursting into womanhood.

One of those who near her stand
Lifts the lifeless rigid hand,

And a crimson-tinted rose
Bursting from its shroud of green,
With a lily wrapt in snows,
Lays her breast and hand between.
One with beauty yet unshown,
Fitting emblem of her own ;
One from darker tinting free,
Emblem of her purity.

These retire, the pall is spread,
Earth reclaims the early dead ;
Mourning ones the maiden bear
To her narrow chamber cold,
Lay the treasured ashes there,
Gently place the sacred mould.
Summer's morning rays serene
Light the hallowed mound of green,
And her ev'ning breezes sigh
Whispered dirges, passing by.

Autumn shuts the summer flow'r
Blooming at too late an hour ;
But a veil of golden air
For the lovely sleeper weaves,

Spreads with fairy fingers there
Robes of purple-tinted leaves.
Winter, fearing that his blast
Might awake her sweeping past,
For protection, o'er her throws
Mantles of his drifting snows.

Spring, with touch of fingers light,
Lays aside the robes of white ;
Bending o'er the naked mound,
Smooths again the crumbling mould,
O'er its bosom, cold and browned,
Spreads her vernal mantle's fold,
Scatters wildwood flowerets,
Tiny vines and violets,
Decks their buds with gems at even,
Mirroring the lamps of heaven.

The Silent City.

BESIDE the sea a silent city stands :
　　In child-like glee the waters at its feet
Heap up the pebbles with their busy hands,
　　And half aloud some well-known song repeat.
Some homes the marble richly carved display,
　　And some the roughly hewn moss-covered stone,
Some show but wood half-eaten by decay,
　　And some are roofed with common turf alone.
Near some, the fir with beck'ning hand is seen
　　To lure to it each straying breath of air,
And flowers lay aside their robes of green
　　And to the breeze their fragrant breasts unbare.
Near some, the knotty shrub and briar grow
　　So close their tangled tresses interlace,
And weeds so thick that none would ever know
　　Here lies concealed a human dwelling-place.

Its homes are silent.　Not a whisper breaks
　　The lasting spell of quietness profound ;

Nor Music e'er the hand of Dancing takes
  To lead her swiftly through the mazy round.
The prattling of the infant's lisping tongue,
  The maiden's voice as sweet as tinkling rill,
The strong and manly accents of the young,
  The trembling voices of the old, are still.

They all are homes of rest.   From street to street
  No sound of busy toil, no hurried tread ;
To chase the phantom, Wealth, no restless feet,
  No hands to struggle wildly but for bread.
No troubled dreams to mar their slumber deep,
  No fevered cheeks, no limbs that toss in pain,
No weary eyes that close but find no sleep,
  No grief-swept breast, no burning madd'ning brain.

The tott'ring aged, wearied from their day
  Of toil, here come and lay them down to rest ;
Here come the rosy children from their play,
  And sinks to quiet slumber every breast.
Here come the gay, the sad, the child of health,
  The sick one racked with more than mortal throes,
The noble, base, the pampered son of wealth,
  The tattered wretch,—and all find sweet repose.

Theirs is oblivious rest.   The silent bride
  With smiles the coming bridegroom never greets ;
The child down-nestling at its mother's side
  No clasping arm, nor word of welcome meets.
They never mark the beauty's flowing tress,
  Her lustrous eye, the bloom upon her cheek ;
The lips of him that loved her never press
  In fondness hers, nor of her praises speak.
Here friend by friend will come to seek repose,
  And never recognize the loved one near ;
Here, side by side, lie down the bitterest foes,
  Forgetful of their former rage and fear.
All, wearied in their search, in endless train,
  From lisping babe to sire with hoary head,
Come here to seek for rest, nor seek in vain,—
  This is a silent City of the Dead.

A Dream at Eventide.

Now lonely at coming of ev'ning I stray
  To grove, and on flowers reclining,
I watch the sun's golden-illumining ray
  On argent-bright vapor clouds shining.

They seem, as they float in the opaline air,
  Like islands in purple seas lying,
Bright Isles of the Blest, all radiant and fair,
  With beauty and verdure ne'er dying.

The purple hue on the horizon now fades,
  The tints from cloud-islands effacing;
And all the dusk air of the even invades,
  The earth in soft lustre embracing.

Then noiselessly through the blue regions on high
  Invisible angel ones glancing,
Rekindle the scintillant lamps of the sky,
  Resplendent with glory entrancing.

Their tremulous rays of innocuous light
    They cast in an earthly direction,
And find in the crystalline dews of the night
    A brilliant and changing reflection.

And with the cool breezes that blow through these
        bow'rs
    Of beauty and fragrance, is blending
The odorous incense of radiant flow'rs
    From numberless censers ascending.

Before me in shrouded and shadow-forms, fast
    The friends of my lifetime are thronging ;
Some loved ones recalled from the far-distant past,
    And some to the present belonging.

Apart from the other loved ones, there appears
    In columned and flower-twined portal,
An angel-like form of the ne'er-forgot years,
    Enrobed in a beauty immortal.

Her brow, finely moulded, vines waving reveal,
    Encrowned by her dark-flowing tresses,
And buds lily-white strive its beauty to steal
    By gentle incessant caresses.

6

The roses, forgetting their own lovely hue,
  Extending from pendulous cluster,
Endeavor by touching her cheek to imbue
  Their leaves with its delicate lustre.

But when to my bosom her form I enclasp,
  Her features grow white as the lily,
And lifeless and cold turns the hand that I grasp,
  Her fingers grow rigid and chilly;

The form is enwrapt in a shadowy shroud,
  The hands on the bosom are folded,
And formless and indistinct vapors encloud
  The features that Beauty had moulded.

I start from my rest on the flowerets fair,
  With night-dews of crystal now laden,
But fancy I see in the shade-mingled air
  The eyes of the vanishing maiden.

My grief-burdened heart is warmed with delight
  By feeling that she in a vision
Thus often returns from her dwelling-place bright
  In e'er-blooming valleys elysian.

In Palliation.

When ev'ning's filmy curtain slow descends,
  And Silence comes his lonely watch to keep;
When queenly Night, star-jewelled, lowly bends
  To guard the earth enwrapped in dewy sleep;

While for a time my eyes forget to close,
  And gaze entranced upon these beauties rare,
A figure suddenly its presence shows,
  And lends a charm to every beauty there.

When Slumber slowly drops his opiate veils,
  She seems to close my eyes with ling'ring hand,
E'en when I stray in Dreamland's misty dales,
  Near every grove or fount I see *her* stand.

But chide me not because this form appears
  To leave an impress more endeared than all
That cluster round my heart from other years,
  That mem'ry never wearies to recall;

For has not Beauty lent her charms divine—
   And lacks she any needed art to please?
Is not her motion as of pendent vine
   That dallies with the wanton ev'ning breeze?

Is not her brow in purer light arrayed
   Than that which bathes the brow of marble saint,
When morning beams have through the chancel
     strayed
   With sunny hand the columned aisles to paint?

And has not Fancy whispered that her eyes
   The pureness of the light within bespeak;
That autumn leaves have lent their varied dyes
   To tint the color on her lip and cheek?

And if that friend seemed so enchanting then
   That still her form seems ever near to mine;
If mem'ry loves to bring that form again,
   Pray do not chide me, for the form is—thine.

The Star.

WHILE walking in half-lighted shadow
  That wrapped me in days long ago,
There shone on my path for a moment
  A star of a wonderful glow—
A glow that was strangely entrancing,
  A glow so peculiarly bright
My soul seemed to start in my bosom
  To bask in the crystalline light;
A star that, though plainly of heaven,
  Seemed nearer and nearer to shine—
So near that it seemed I might clasp it
  And claim it forever as mine.

It shone but a moment and vanished;
  I watched with unwearying eyes
Till over my path, full of splendor,
  That star once again should arise.
It came in its lustre unfaded;
  I followed wherever it led;
The mystical valleys of Dreamland
  I trod by the light that it shed.

But sudden a cloud rose, obscuring
  And hiding its soul-cheering light,
And left me unguided, bewildered,
  In deep cypress shadows of night.
The cloud raised its towers of darkness,
  And higher its ramparts upreared ;
Methought that behind it forever
  In gloom had my star disappeared.
I thought it had left me to wander
  The valley deep-shadowed and lone,
With naught but the dim light of mem'ry
  To guide through the windings unknown.

The clouds passed away, and I noticed
  A tremulous beaming afar ;
My bosom half trustingly whispered,
  " Perchance 'tis a ray from thy star."
I gazed, half believing the whisper,
  Till fled all my doubtings away ;
For nearer the star seemed approaching,
  And clearer and brighter its ray.
It seemed with such love-breathing radiance
  So near and so warmly to shine,
It waked my sad soul from its slumber,
  And warmed this cold bosom of mine.

Oh ! say what mysterious power,
   What spell o'er my soul has this star ?
What links with invisible fetters
   My soul to that being afar ?
When darkened, my breast is a prison
   In which my soul wretchedly pines ;
My soul finds that bosom a palace
   When brightly and warmly it shines.
I know, when upon me no longer
   That love-breathing look shall descend,
This dream we call Life shall be over,
   My day upon earth be at end.

Encouragement.

SKIES had doffed the gold of morning
    And their sable garments worn,
Burdens light had chafed my shoulders,
    Little thorns my feet had torn.

Wearied, down beside the pathway
    Fretfully myself I flung,
Thinking life's way rough and toilsome,
    E'er with darkness overhung.

Suddenly came Mem'ry, tripping
    As a bright-lipped, fair-browed maid ;
Smiling, down she knelt beside me
    And in mine her hand she laid.

" Is the sky *e'er* dark ? " she whispered,
    " *All* the way so rough and drear ?
Come and backward let us ramble,
    Leave awhile your burdens here."

Hand in hand we rambled backward
   Till we reached a deep ravine ;
On its sides the trees were standing
   In their gayest robes of green.

'Through its depths a stream came tripping
   Swift along its winding banks,
Leaping over rocks and dancing,
   Laughing at its idle pranks.

O'er it trees their hands extended,
   From the sun its breast to screen,
But the sun their wide-spread fingers
   Shot his golden shafts between.

Mem'ry whispered to me, "Surely,
   Surely here your feet have strayed ;
Here you stood and watched the streamlet
   As among the rocks it played ;

" *Here* you climbed the rugged pathway
   Leading to the ruined mill ;
Here you bent and saw the mighty
   Wheel with giant arms, was still ;

" *Here* between two rugged boulders
    Hastily a seat you made,
Where you sat and gazed enraptured
    On the silver-tongued cascade.

" Surely now you cannot tell me
    All the way is rough and drear,
E'er the sky is wrapped in darkness—
    Were they so when you were here ?"

And then smiling Mem'ry, turning,
    Whispered as a zephyr low,
Lest the list'ning trees around us
    Might from her the secret know.

" It is she who wandered with you
    On that eve to this ravine ;
She whose eyes with yours so fondly
    Rested on the treasured scene ;

" She who with you watched the streamlet,
    With you at the ruin bent,
With you sat upon the boulders,
    That to all the charm has lent."

Then we slow retraced our footsteps,
    But the sun in beauty shone ;
All the way seemed smooth before me,
    And I found my burdens gone.

On Receiving a Long-Promised Box of Flowers.

THIS box of newly·bursting blooms
    For long delay will make amends,
Their fragrance sweet that all perfumes
    Is like the heart of her that sends.

These verdant vines, that tendrils fling
    And clasp the tinted blooms around,
Are like her heart, that close will cling
    Where aught that's pure and fair is found.

And every tint that lightly warms
    Or flushes golden cup with flame,
Is emblem of a heart that charms
    And sheds a brightness just the same.

Question and Answer.

You ask if I, when youth has turned to age,
    Can love you still though youthful bloom be gone ;
If I, when morn is past and ev'ning near,
    Can love the dark'ning ev'ning as the dawn ;

If I shall ruthless spurn the drooping stem
    When buds of spring and summer flowers rare
And autumn's golden fruits have been and gone,
    And winter finds it beauty-robbed and bare.

The sailor may his new-built vessel prize
    When first she launches on the waters blue,
Unfurls her spotless canvas to the breeze,
    And cleaves a foamy path the billows through ;

But he will prize that gallant vessel more,
    Although her sails be rent and weather-stained,
When she has proudly braved the tempest's rage
    And safely has the destined harbor gained.

I shall not ruthless spurn the drooping stem
   If op'ning bud shall bring the promised flow'r,
If opened flow'r to promised fruit shall turn,
   Though naked found in winter's chilly hour.

But if those buds remain forever closed ;
   If fruit and flower never spring from them,
But jagged thorns and withered leaves instead,
   Who would not spurn the naked, worthless stem ?

If ev'ning have the morning's balmy airs,
   Though golden tints may not the skies adorn,
If stinging blasts do not my bosom pierce,
   I then shall love the ev'ning as the morn.

I'll love you still though lustrous eye may dim,
   Though cheek may pale and burning lip grow cold,
If trusting heart remain—for who would scorn
   A gem because the casket had grown old ?

Your outward graces are not what I prize,
   But yet I do not deem them valueless,
For does not Nature teach us lovely forms
   Are far more lovely in becoming dress ?

Cheek beauty fades ; heart beauty never can.
    Heart beauty has its mirror in the face ;
And so we ever fondly hope to find
    The inner when we have the outer grace.

But if, when age shall blanch your cheek and lip,
    And steal the youthful lustre from your eyes,
There shall be found no warm and loving heart,
    What *will* remain that I *can* love or prize ?

In the Sunny Land of Youth.

In the sunny land of Youth
    Gather gems thy form to grace
While their path through Womanhood
    Thy advancing feet must trace—
Purity, thy brow to light ;
    Modesty, to grace thy neck ;
Truth, to sparkle on thy breast ;
    Charity, thy hand to deck.
Cheek may pale and eye grow dim,
    Burning lip of youth grow cold,
But these gems will keep thee fair
    Though by years thou mayst be old.

A Fragile Vase is in Your Hand.

A FRAGILE vase is in your hand,
   Weeds on your path with flowers grow,
And you must gather as you pass
   To fill this spotless vase of snow.

Then pluck not vile offensive weeds,
   But choose the fragrant buds and rare ;
No faded flow'r or lurking weed
   Should mar the clusters gathered there.

For they're to deck the home of One
   That waits the coming of your feet,
And will, if all be fresh and fair,
   With loving smile your coming greet.

Oft When Weary are Our Feet.

OFT when weary are our feet
    Flowers by the way appear,
Buds and bloom with perfume sweet
    Laden, weary hearts to cheer.

Friends have I on life's way met,
    Sent like these to cheer the heart—
Flowers by the wayside set—
    Mary, such a one thou art.

•
———————

True Friendship is a Golden Chain.

TRUE friendship is a golden chain
    That links the faithful hearted,
And life is only sweet when yet
    The linklets have not parted.

We leave the world with scarce a sigh,
    And ne'er a murmur spoken,
When every link is snapped in twain,
    Or all the dearest broken.

May Life for Thee be One Continual Song.

May life for thee be one continual song
    That in the morning shall recall thy feet
From Dreamland's never-ending paths, where throng
    The loved and ne'er-forgot thy steps to meet.
A cheery song, that in the noontide's glare
    Shall free thy breast from every throb of pain,
Hush in thy breast, at eve, the voice of care,
    And all the night breathe out its sweet refrain—
A song with *constant* strains that, soft'ning, tell
    If e'er the kindly ray has been withdrawn ;
Not such as fitfully exulting swell
    From organ lips a moment, and are gone.

May all thy life be as a limpid stream—
    Now in the meadow's richest sunlight dressed ;
Now gliding 'neath the boughs where noontide's beam
    Yet scatters golden network o'er its breast.
A stream that will, if nearing chilly glen,
    But hush its song where ebon Shadow spreads

His gloomy wing, then gaily sing again
· When all is sunshine o'er its pebbly beds.
A stream which ripples calmly to the sea,
   And, ent'ring, still keeps an unruffled breast,
Then onward glides, from every tossing free,
   To golden sands and isles of perfect rest.

A Wish.

MAY fairy hands for thee thy path prepare
   Where all life's darker shadows never rest,
Clear streams repeat a sweetly murmured air
   To rocking buds yet cradled on their breast,
June's blossomed roses breathe their lives away
   To airs that wanton with their tiny lips,
The morning ne'er withdraw its cheery ray
   Or fairest scene enshroud in dark eclipse.
Delight unfading may the present bring,
   An amaranthine lustre robe the past,
The future yield the promised joys of spring,
   And calm eternal rest be thine at last.

Friendship.

HEART linked to heart by friendship's chain,
  Both every shock receiving,
No piercing shaft the one can pain
  Without the other grieving.

The joy that lightens one will fill
  The other too with gladness ;
So linked that both with joy must thrill,
  Or both must bleed in sadness.

A chain that use wears not away,
  But more enduring makes it ;
A chain so strong that none can say
  That even death quite breaks it.

And yet, the linklets of this chain
  A hasty word may sever ;
And they, if parted once, again
  Are rarely joined, if ever.

Each Flower to Heaven Upturns its Eye.

EACH flow'r to heaven upturns its eye
    And constant gazing stands;
The tiny vines that lowly lie
    Yet heav'nward lift their hands.

Their fragrant souls in death arise
    And float to heaven too;
O can they know of fairer skies
    Beyond the dome of blue?

And are they dumbly pointing man
    The way to realms of bliss,
And showing where pure spirits can
    Find fairer worlds than this?

No Tasks Thy God hath Given Thee.

No tasks thy God hath given thee
    Can I to thee unfold ;
And did I know, perchance 'twere best
    To leave them still untold.
For, knowing what those tasks would be,
    Thy hands might listless fall,
And thou the moments fret away
    And leave unfinished all.
But thinking each to be the last
    Thou'lt finish one by one,
And calmly fold thy hands to rest
    And know thy work is done.

The Poet's Office.

Tossing jewels in the sunlight
  Till they glow and gleam ;
Till they show the hues of glory
Caught in limpid depths of ocean,
  Sunlit brook or frozen stream ;
Till the green and golden flamings
Caught from earth-hid smouldering masses
Where the hand of nature formed them,
  Blaze again with flash and beam.

Holding flowers till their odors
  As from swinging censer rise,
Odors borne by sea-born breezes
Wand'ring over starlit meadows,
  Where the flower sleeping lies ;
Till they show the varied colors
Left by tinted trailing vestments
Of the swiftly fleeting rainbow,
  Or the flaming ev'ning skies.

Hushing all the world to listen
　To the rich and varied tones,
When the boughs bend low to whisper
Love to streams that sweetly answer,
　Murm'ring 'mid their mossy stones ;
When the meadows and the woodlands
Ring with the minstrels of the morning ;
When the organ voice of Ocean
　Swells, or sinks in plaintive moans.

Holding Truth till all her glory
　To the human eye is clear ;
Till before her light of splendor
All the varied forms of error,
　Doubt and darkness disappear ;
Till the wrongs of men are righted,
Till all human hearts are moulded
To the image of their Maker,
　Bringing earth to heaven near.

A Child Asleep in the Gardens.

THE SCENE.

THE hush of eve lies on the land,
   A summer ev'ning when no breeze
Dare lightly lift its fairy hand
   To touch in love the slumb'ring trees;
But silent floods of silver fall,
   Outlining deftly leaf and spray,
Till mossy mound and turf and all,
   The richest arabesque display.
Each flow'ret finds its image there,
   And breathless and bewildered stands,
Entrancèd like a maiden fair,
   With bowèd head and claspèd hands.
The urns upon the level lawn,
   Or where the branches lowly sweep,
Their robes of trailing vines have drawn
   About their shapely forms and sleep.
In snowy robes of slumber bow
   The graceful marble forms, or raise

The glowing pure unshrinking brow
 With breast unbared to Heaven's gaze.
The fountain, too, repose has found ;
 The nymphs that sported all the day
With curving jets the basin round,
 Have sunk in slumber where they lay ;
Or, gaze at forms of graceful mould
 That in the limpid waters lie,
Or, far below, where gems and gold
 Have sunk in falling from the sky.

THE DISCOVERY.

But one in clinging robes of white,
 Apart upon a mossy mound,
Has toyed with fragrant blooms and bright
 Till fast in slumber-fetters bound.
The lily sleeps upon her brow,
 The rose is slumb'ring on her cheek,
And wine is on her lips that now
 Seem parting slightly as to speak.
The richness of each flowing tress
 Is half by twining circlet hid ;
And, clothed in darkness, closely press
 The fringes of each folded lid.

Moss-pillowed cheek, snow-moulded arms
   That bending blooms caress and kiss,
Mere marble never had such charms,
   Nor chisel shaped a form like this.

THE RECOGNITION.

My Mary, thou hast slumbered long,
   With dews thy loosened locks are wet;
The last lone bird has hushed its song,
   And, loved one, thou art slumb'ring yet.
Awake, for one by one the stars
   On tiptoe from their homes in air,
Have stolen out to heaven's bars,
   And downward gaze in wonder there.
Awake, for daylight long is gone,
   Thy bank of fragrant blooms forsake;
The midnight swift is stealing on,
   Awake, my love—my love, awake.

Thoughtlessness.

A ROSEBUD in a sunbeam's arms
  In sweet repose was sleeping,
Its tiny face with cheek of pink
  From hood of green was peeping.

The sunbeam gazed upon the rose,
  And fondly he caressed it,
But bruised its tender lip, as he
  With kiss too ardent pressed it.

And though he softly bathed the wound,
  Though Night, with tears, him aided,
In life, and e'en in death, the scar
  Still never, never faded.

Thus, thoughtless, we may bruise a heart,
  And earnestly endeavor
To heal the wound, but, as the rose,
  It wears the scar forever.

The Girls of Demill.

O who has not heard of the girls of Demill,
And felt in his heart, when they're mentioned, a
    thrill !
If I were but gifted I'd talk of their charms—
Of queen-like proportions, of snow-moulded arms,
Of pink-tinted fingers and little white hands
That hold us more firmly than triple steel bands ;
I'd talk of their tresses of raven or gold
That Graces and Loves in their meshes enfold ;
I'd speak of the wealth of affection that lies
Enshrined in the depths of their warm lustrous eyes ;
Of cheeks that are dimpled and mantled with bloom ;
Of lips slightly parted, affording but room
For musical words so enchantingly sweet
They make of our bosoms the conquest complete.
But who, let him struggle and strive as he will,
Can paint half the charms of the girls of Demill ?

These outward attractions have girls of Demill,
But their inward adornments are lovelier still.

With richest of jewels, with gold thrice refined,
With rarest of treasures they're storing the mind ;
They're waking to life in the depths of the breast
Its purest affections, its noblest and best ;
They're training the hand with the requisite skill
Behests of the mind and the heart to fulfil,
For delicate hand should be ever the best
To charm away pain, or relieve the distressed.
Though flash of bright eye and the dark flowing tress
May move me to feel more than tongue can express,
Yet give me the treasure of heart and of mind—
The outer may *win*, but the inner will *bind ;*
The glow of the cheek and the eye may depart,
But the glow never fades from a warm loving heart.
You'll shine with the outer one, go where you will,
But neglect not the inner, dear girls of Demill.

Address to a Mummy Cat.

Say, did life's flick'ring taper shine
Within this withered frame of thine,
These limbs, now fettered, freedom know
So many centuries ago?
Has Ruin strewn with cities vast
The desert valleys of the Past,
And hidden with the dust of Time
Their temples grand and halls sublime;
And art *thou* left, a thing of clay,
To mock the fingers of Decay?
Come, tell us how thy life was spent.
When didst thou live, where didst thou dwell,
What purpose had the hands that pent
Thy form in spices, canst thou tell?
Shall naught of thee be ever known
Beyond what here to us is shown?
And canst thou not thy *tail* unfold?
Or did their dusky fingers fail
To find a way to fold thy tail,
And so, this task to obviate,
Thy loved appendage amputate?

Wast thou esteemed a thing divine
And kept within a gilded shrine,
Where priests in flowing robes arrayed
With sacred hands thy food prepared,
Their off'rings on thine altar laid
And for thy every comfort cared?
And hast thou listened and looked wise,
Or sat with listless, half-closed eyes,
Or slow thy whiskered jaws caressed,
While they to thee their prayers addressed?

Perchance thou wast no sacred cat,
But some birth-proud aristocrat
That by the stately rolling·Nile   •
Dwelt in some noble marble pile,
Whose chiseled frieze and colonnade
The morning beams in gold arrayed,
Whose mighty pillars shone at night
With softer but yet purer light,
When dallying breezes in her bow'rs
By moonlight flirted with the flow'rs.
Didst thou within these marble walls
    With stately bearing make thy way,
Or caper through the sculptured halls
    Regardless of the grand array?

When wearied, did these limbs of thine
On richly 'broidered couch recline?
Did liv'ried menials on thee wait?
Wast thou a loved associate
Of proudest ladies of the land?
   And hast thou arched thy back when praised, .
   Thy vertebral extension raised
To meet the touch of jewelled hand?

Or, wast thou once the joy and pride
   Of some rude hut whose occupants,
Though famine-threatened, ne'er denied
   Their store to satisfy thy wants?
And has the matron ceased awhile
   From toil, to watch thee at thy play,
And have thy antics caused a smile
   Across her care-worn face to stray?
Perchance the rugged sire who spent
   His days to meet Want's stern demand,
At ev'ning's quiet hour has bent
   To stroke thee with toil-hardened hand;
His saddened face grown bright to see
   Thy rompings with his dark-eyed child,
That bloomed amid his poverty
   As flow'ret 'mid a desert wild.

Did she with thee her dainties share,
  And ere she well thy weight could raise,
Love in her arms thy form to bear,
Thy heels above, thy head below,
 And in such strange unheard-of ways
As only cats and children know?
Didst thou to the indignity
Submit when, having tried to free
  Thyself from her encircling clasp,
Just as thou hadst thy freedom found
And from her wast about to bound,
  Her hand thy luckless tail would grasp?
Or, with a rude grimalkin oath
  Didst thou thy quick release demand,
And strike thy claws with all thy force
  In thy tormentor's dusky hand?

Wast thou despised by humankind,
And forced by hunger's pangs to find
The sustenance that man denied,
Where chance thy stealthy steps would guide?
Wast thou a fugitive that fled
From death and every nameless dread
  To wandering grimalkin known?
   8

A vagrant, roaming at its will,
Whose life depended on its skill
   In shunning missiles at it thrown?
A pugilist, that loved to stray
In dark and noisome lanes by day;
That left at night its foul retreat
To prowl around the lonely street;
That loved to give the battle-cry
If other cat came wand'ring nigh,
And shrouded by night's ebon veils,
   Down on its hated foe to sweep?
(A conflict grim which seemed a heap
Of scratching claws and lashing tails;)
That loved, e'en when the dread embrace
Was broken, still to sit and face
Its foe, and make Egyptian halls
Re-echo with its caterwauls.

And, when none dared with thee engage,
Didst thou survive to honored age,
And cats around thee crowd to hear
The triumphs great of thy career,
Then go, inspired by deeds of fame,
To strive to win as great a name?

Or, did at last some stronger foe
In deadly combat lay thee low?
And, dying, didst thou strive in vain
To win thy laurels back again,
And, e'en in death, thy foe defy
With starting claw and glaring eye,
Which seemed to show the stubborn will
Within thee was unconquered still?
Did men a noted warrior brave
Allow to have but such a grave
As common herd of cats can crave,
 Which lie and bleach their weary bones
 On wayside heap of sticks and stones,
Or sink with brickbats 'neath the wave?
Nay, thou must be in spices pent
To be a lasting monument
To show to modern fighters bold
What fame grimalkins won of old.

Wast thou of scientific bent,
And didst thou, after having spent
Long time in studious privacy,
Discover Darwin's theory?
And, prompted by that strange desire
For state of being somewhat higher,

By much deep musing form the plan
  To wrap thyself in this cocoon,
  Expecting to *develop* soon,
And proudly walk the earth, A MAN ?

If thou wilt not thy station tell,
Nor what strange chances thee befell,
  But meetst with stubborn silence all,
Come, lay these linen wrappings by,
Shake from thy form the dust of years,
Uplift thy loved extension high,
And greet, at least, our anxious ears
  With true Egyptian caterwaul.

"Cash" McLeod.

WHEN sunlight has faded and darkness o'ershaded
   The earth with invisible veil ;
When lamp is low burning and lovers are yearning
   To whisper the ever new tale ;
When sighs are the longest and vows are the strongest,
   Then be not too hasty or rash.
In spite of their sighing they may be just lying ;
Be watchful and wary, they're all mercenary,
   They're certainly coming for "Cash."

O happy the mortal who will through the portal
   Of bliss with thee wander and say,
Just as a cloud guided the Jews undecided,
   McLeod (my cloud) too is *my* guide by day.
Though fortunes unending in ruin descending
   'Round heads of their owners may crash,
I'll feel no dejection, but seek thy direction,
And all the way dreary I'll keep a heart cheery,
   And hug my plump bundle of "Cash."

To Matilda Robins.

THE nature of thy character
We may well from thy name infer,
   And call thee, too, a robin ;
For when first through the veil of night
There comes a promised ray of light,
The robin bursts in song to cheer
The drooping hearts of all that hear,
And forces gloom to disappear,
   And so dost thou, Matilda.

I pray thy dwelling e'er may be
Where fragrant flow'r and shady tree
   Are found, as is the robin's.
And if to grace that cheery home
A little group of nestlings come,
O be—there is no higher aim,
No lip a sweeter word can frame,
None can a prouder title claim—
   O be a true Ma, 'Tilda.

May all thy sad and cheerless hours
As quickly pass as summer show'rs
   That fall upon the robin.

When comrades of the grove are fled,
And ling'ring flow'rets all are dead ;
When cold and piercing blasts betray
The coming of the wintry day,
To fairer climes it flits away,
 And so shalt thou, Matilda.

An Acrostic.

KNOW that concealed within these lines there lies
 The name of one whom all that know hold dear,
Within the artless depths of whose bright eyes
 A true heart's lovelinesses all appear.
Might I for her through life a pathway make,
 Nought would I spare of what would charm or please;
With blooms her path I'd scatter for her sake
 And lade with odors every passing breeze.
Through verdant fields, by winding streams her way
Should enter into realms of endless day.

  KEY.—Take first letter of first word of first line : take second letter of
second word of second line ; take third letter of third word of third line, etc.,
until a word is formed, then begin over again.

Johnny Science and his Late Discovery at the North Pole.

IN eighteen and ten, in the month of November,
As near as the neighboring folk can remember,
Was born, in an out-of-the-way little village,
The son of a doctor who lived by his *pill*age.
This wonderful infant was known by the name
Of Johnny, and even before he could frame
His words of ten syllables, ever was tasking
The patience of father and mother by asking
Such questions as these : " If to walk flies are able
Because they have legs, then why cannot the table ?
If men walk on two legs, why cannot a fly ?"
And he'd pull out its legs to induce it to try.
He thought it unjust bugs and flies should have wings,
While none had the spiders, the dear little things ;
So he'd catch bugs and flies wherever he spied 'em
And pull off their wings and proceed to divide 'em.
His father ne'er thought these performances cruel,
But went on compounding his pills and his gruel ;

And pounded while thinking, and thought while com-
    pounding,
These actions of Johnny's were very astounding.

As Johnny grew older the world, too, grew wider ;
He spent not his time upon fly, bug, or spider ;
His passion now led him to orchards surrounding
To see whether apples and pears were abounding ;
And it seemed that the fellow the fact never knew
Until he had seen them and tasted them too.
John Newton, that apples came down by attraction
    Had found on that day when *he* went out of town ;
But Johnny, far wiser, with great satisfaction,
    Soon found 'cos he hit 'em the apples came down.

The years sped away, and this John was e'er gaining
In knowledge, and now was his manhood attaining.
No longer he thought of pears, apples or vermin,
But turned his attention to Latin and German,
And Hebrew and Greek, and to French and to
    Spanish,
Italian and Russian, Arabian, Danish,
To Chinese and Japanese, Turkish and Choctaw,
And horrible ones that 'most gave him the lockjaw.

In fact, every language that ever was known
This Johnny had mastered, *excepting his own.*
He studied Zoology, also Geology,
Anthropomorphology, Meteorology,
And ancient Astrology, Paleontology,
And Paley's Theology, and each other *ology.*
He read Pyronomics, profound Mathematics,
Dynamics, and Hydrodynamics, and Statics,
Acoustics and Optics, Dioptics, Pneumatics,
Chromatics and Physics, and deep Hydrostatics,
Cosmology, Alchemy, Chemistry, Botany,
Astronomy, Logic—in fact there was not any
Frightful-named science or art you could mention
To which this same John hadn't given attention.
Abstruse Metaphysics this Johnny was versed in,
And never became he so deeply immersed in
The deep muddy seas of his own speculation
That *he* couldn't see out, nor a man in creation.

Of all of the theories science propounded,
By one, only *one,* was our Johnny confounded.
He found that astronomers even pretended
To say that the world was on *nothing* suspended.

" They e'er of *attraction* and *forces* are prating.
These cannot support it ; I found out, while skating,
   My body, if left unsupported, came down.
The earth's is much larger, more weighty. Conceive it
Not falling !   I cannot, I will not believe it,"
   Impatiently Johnny would say with a frown.
He thought—he *thought ?*   Why, he e'en boldly con-
   tended
The earth in some way by the Poles was suspended.
The word " pole " itself implied this explanation,
Else why should the place have this strange appella-
   tion ?
But lest the astronomers ever should doubt it,
He'd prove he was right—and at once set about it.

The Pole must be reached ; but he saw expeditions
Sent thither had failed to accomplish their missions.
He saw in the fact that the wrong means were taken,
The reason why each had the journey forsaken.
These warnings from blunders of others he heeded ;
He saw that three things for the journey were needed—
Provisions and *warmth,* means of *safe locomotion*
O'er icebergs and floes of the cold Polar Ocean.

The problem of food was the first he propounded,
And soon with a wonderful skill he compounded
A Double-concentrated Patent Elixir,
One bottle of which would supply twenty-six or
Eight men with abundance of means of sustaining
Life's taper as long as a spark was remaining.
Now warmth was the next thing, and quickly dis-
    cerning
The fact that *within* fires are constantly burning,
He thought if he only could check radiation
This heat were enough to prevent congelation.
He then set to work at the thing that was needed,
And soon beyond all expectation succeeded.
He made an enveloping suit, in construction
So perfect it wholly prevented conduction :
Heat couldn't get out, for this Johnny compelled it
To stay like a bird in the prison that held it.

A safe means of travelling must next be provided,
And he soon on his mode of procedure decided.
Of course, he'd encounter rough ice-fields unnum-
    bered,
But would not with sledges and tools be encumbered ;
For others, when they would obstructions discover,

Must hew their way through them, but he would pass
  over.
As climbing o'er ice was with danger attended,
One mounted quite slow, and oft quickly descended,
He a Glacier Adhesive not long was providing,
Which, applied to the feet, would check slipping and
  sliding.

Equipped thus at last to his own satisfaction,
He started one spring for the ice-fields of action.
He toiled on his way, and long before reaching
The Pole there arose such a horrible screeching,
And trembling, and sighing, and mumbling, and
  moaning,
And whizzing, and whirring, and creaking, and
  groaning,
And clanking, and roaring, and rumbling, and
  shaking,
And grinding, and grating, and crashing, and
  quaking,
As if all machines, all the old rusty-growing
Concerns upon earth, in confusion were going;
While near horrid demons the chorus were swelling
By shrieking and clanking their fetters and yelling.

So frightened was John, he, with all of his yearning
For knowledge, was once on the point of returning.
His teeth went like shutters in bad windy weather;
His knees, like two drumsticks, were knocking to-
    gether;
The hair on his head (for the noise so appalled one)
Would have stood up on end, had it not been a bald
    one.
But willing to be a true martyr to Science,
He bade all his foes, since there were none, defiance,
And conquered his fears, and then onward proceeded;
And nothing appeared or his journey impeded
Till when on the top of a hill he ascended
He saw that his toil with success was attended.
Before him arose such a scene as no vision
Reveals to a mortal in Dreamland elysian.
A feeling of awe blent with rapture came o'er him
While gazing on what none had witnessed before him;
For there stood the Pole, and two shafts were ex-
    tending
Away in the distance—shafts seeming unending.
On one he saw standing a giant-like being,
With man in his form and his features agreeing.
His well-moulded form so gigantic he seeming

Might grasp the bright stars which above him were
    gleaming.
His arms were like pillars of iron unbending ;
His hair like a cloud on his shoulders descending ;
The lines on his brow were like clefts of the moun-
    tain
Out-worn by the storm or the swift-running fountain.
He turned the great shaft over which he was bending,
To naught in the least but his labor attending.

John saw that the shaft caused the earth's revolution,
The moon's round the earth—it afforded solution,
He afterwards found, of the earth's yearly motions,
Completely o'erturning astronomers' notions.
Machinery used and the mode of its action
May be seen in the drawing with more satisfaction.
By levers, omitted for obvious reasons,
Were managed such things as eclipses and seasons.
This shaft (*a*) our John mounted without trepidation
To see if it had or had not termination.
When part of the way he had managed to toil up,
IIe met a strange fellow descending to oil up,
Who asked whence he came, and for what ; and on
    learning

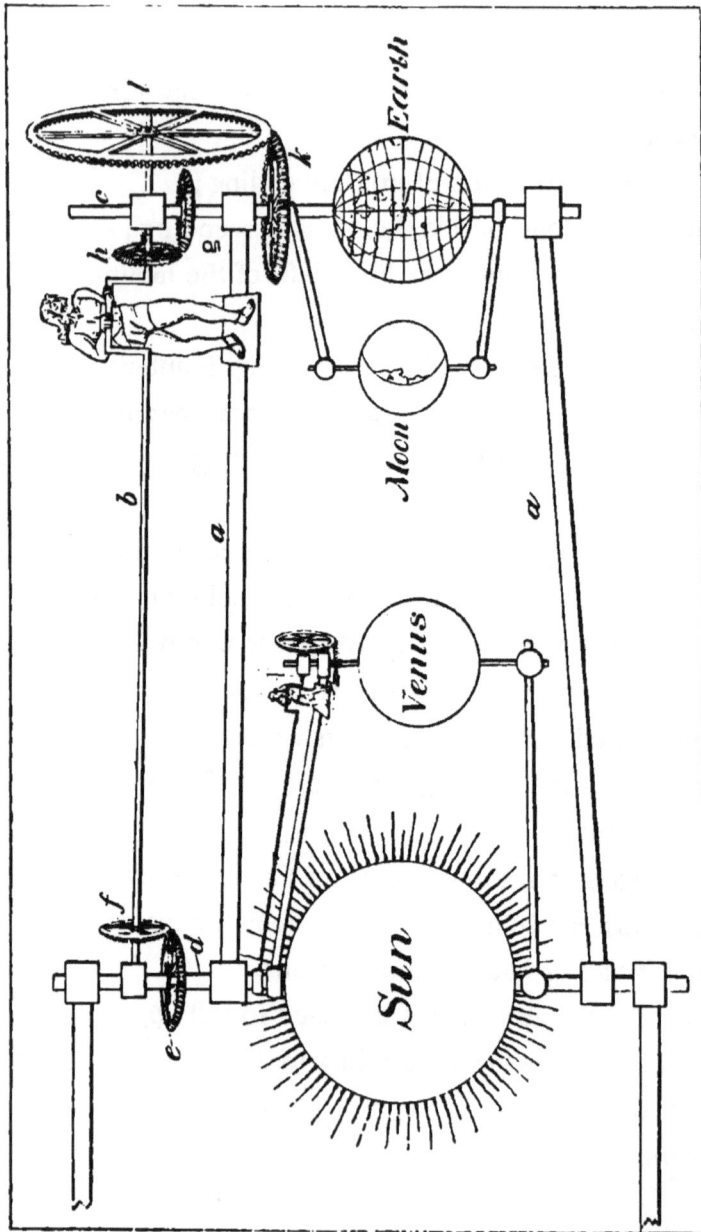

a and *a*, Rigid shafts through the ends of which pole of sun, *d*, and pole of earth, *c*, revolve. *b*, Crank shaft, revolving in boxes on poles. *c*, Cog wheel fixed to shaft *d*. *f*, Pinion wheel fixed to crank shaft, the revolution of which causes earth and moon to travel around the sun. *g*, Cog wheel fixed to pole of earth. *h*, Pinion wheel fixed to crank shaft, the revolution of which causes the earth to revolve on its axis. *k*, Cog wheel revolving on pole of earth and fixed by a shaft to moon. *l*, Cog wheel fixed to crank shaft, the revolution of which causes moon to revolve around earth.

His purpose in climbing advised his returning ;
'Twas warmer up there than he even suspected—
One roasted to cinders if not well protected.
John showed his enveloping suit, in construction
So perfect it wholly prevented conduction.
" Heat cannot get *out*, so if only I turn it,
Heat cannot get *in*, though in furnace you burn
  it."
With sorrow our John all at once recollected
His feet against slipping would not be protected,
His Glacier Adhesive was but for cold weather ;
He must then return—they descended together.
But not that John feared that his life it might cost
  him ;
He thought of the loss to the world if it lost him.

But quickly our John formed the determination
To try from the fellow to get information ;
Who willingly John on the journey conducted,
Explained how the whole thing was worked and con-
  structed,
Explained how the shaft round the sun caused rota-
  tion,
And gave for the planets the same explanation.
  9

The ice and the snow were a happy invention
For keeping things cool, and for friction's prevention.
He said that the wheels, and shafts seeming unending,
Were made from a substance transparent, unbending,
Non-fusible, anti-corrosive, non-frangible,
Hard, non-combustible, acid-intangible,
True anti-friction, resisting attrition,
Contraction, expansion, and torsion and fission.

The time of Creation our John thought of finding
By asking him *when the old man began grinding.*
He willingly gave the much wished information,
And said "He began *at the time of Creation.*"
Undaunted, our John on the point still insisted
By asking how long now the world had existed.
The man now the drift of his question discerning,
Replied, "Ever since the old man has been turning."
John thinks to have settled this old disputation
Alone is worth all of his toil and vexation.

The end of the world our John then thought of finding
By asking how long he'd continue his grinding.
But hearing the axis of Jupiter creaking,
Away went the man with his oil without speaking.

John gazed on his friend as he nimbly departed,
Then hurriedly made his way homeward light-hearted,
But used all his energies ere his descending
To get but a piece of that substance unbending,
Non-fusible, anti-corrosive, non-frangible,
Hard, non-combustible, acid-intangible,
True anti-friction, resisting attrition,
Contraction, expansion, and torsion and fission.
Though active and long in the work he persisted,
Yet still all his efforts the substance resisted.
He thinks it is probable diamonds are needed,
And had he had these that he would have succeeded.
He modestly says that the people who wear them
May *Science* assist if with *him* they will share them.

Results of John's toil are beyond computation :
On planets and moon can be made exploration.
If found well adapted for man's habitation,
And earth should e'er groan with too much popula-
tion,
A part may escape—as we bachelors, beating
About on life's sea, and the rough billows meeting
That dash underneath us, around us, between us,
Escape from our troubles—by flying to VENUS.

www.ingramcontent.com/pod-product-compliance
Lightning Source LLC
Chambersburg PA
CBHW030613270326
41927CB00007B/1160